MW00650063

IMAGES
of America

TRIMPER'S RIDES

Inspired by a visit to Ocean City, Maryland, in 1890, Margaret and Daniel B. Trimper sold their Baltimore bar, the Silver Dollar, to start over in the emerging resort town. By 1904, they would own the entire boardwalk property between South Division and South First Streets. The Trimpers offered their guests entertainment in addition to ocean breezes. The property included a theater, concessions, and an early merry-go-round. (Courtesy of Wendy Bruno-Trimper.)

ON THE COVER: Riders line up on a warm summer evening to experience the chills of the Haunted House created by amusement artist Bill Tracy and ride owner Granville D. Trimper. (Courtesy of the Ocean City Life-Saving Station Museum.)

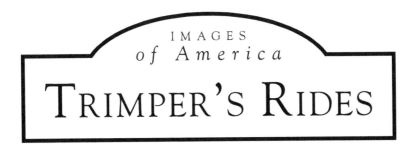

IMAGES
of America

TRIMPER'S RIDES

Monica Thrash and Brandon Seidl

ARCADIA
PUBLISHING

Copyright © 2014 by Monica Thrash and Brandon Seidl
ISBN 978-1-5316-7328-4

Published by Arcadia Publishing
Charleston, South Carolina

Library of Congress Control Number: 2013953050

For all general information, please contact Arcadia Publishing:
Telephone 843-853-2070
Fax 843-853-0044
E-mail sales@arcadiapublishing.com
For customer service and orders:
Toll-Free 1-888-313-2665

Visit us on the Internet at www.arcadiapublishing.com

*To James and Sarah Thrash, who filled my world with books
and taught me that there are always more stories to tell.*

CONTENTS

ACKNOWLEDGMENTS

Monica would like to thank Stephanie Trimper Lewis for her support, encouragement, and gentle mocking; her acquisitions editor, Julia Simpson, for all her patience and support; and Sandy Hurley, Gordon Katz, Bunk Mann, and Diane Knuckles from the Ocean City Museum Society for their insight.

Monica would also like to thank all who shared their memories and images in support of this project, especially Wendy Bruno-Trimper, Wendy DiBuo, Olive Milutin, Brenda Runk Parker, Maria Schlick, Marty Trimper, Doug and Cindy Trimper, Frances Stoneburner, Adam Lewis, Joyce Trimper, Bernie Walls, Linda Holloway, Johnnie Jett, Paul J. Smith, and Jim Futrell

Brandon would like to thank his wife, Stephanie, his parents, David and Patricia, and grandfather William for their continued support, encouragement, and direction through a lifetime of researching and experiencing his greatest passions. Additionally, Brandon would like to thank Chris Trimper, Gordon "Brooks" Trimper, Scott Hudson, Wayne Bahur, and Mike Brilhart for their contributions and insight in support of this project and the development of Trimper's Haunted House Online (www. ochh.net). Unless otherwise noted, all images appear courtesy of the Trimper's Rides archive.

INTRODUCTION

German immigrant Daniel B. Trimper had always possessed an enterprising spirit. While living in Baltimore with his wife, Margaret, he was able to supplement the operation of the family bar, the Silver Dollar, by catering local events, park outings, and boat excursions. Any place people gathered to relax and enjoy themselves seemed another opportunity to provide refreshment and entertainment. When his family visited Ocean City in 1890, the burgeoning town must have seemed to Trimper to be filled with possibilities. The Trimpers bought their first lot in Ocean City in 1892. By 1904, they were owners of the boardwalk property between South Division and South First Streets, including two hotels—the Eastern Shore and the Seabright. The property included a theater for films, boxing, and vaudeville acts; a variety of concessions; and a merry-go-round powered by the strength of two men. When a succession of strong storms damaged the Seabright, the Trimpers rebuilt, ostensibly modeling the new structure on England's Windsor Castle, changing the name to the Windsor, and calling their collection of businesses Windsor Resort.

Trimper was continually adding to his property with new structures and attractions. A 1912 purchase was to bring historic significance to Windsor Resort. It was that year that Daniel Trimper bought a massive carousel (50 feet in diameter) from the Herschell-Spillman Company in North Tonawanda, New York. Its uniqueness was in being one of two carousels of this type made by the firm; the other was sent to Coney Island and was later destroyed by fire. He constructed a new building designed to house the glorious attraction and converted the old merry-go-round house to a lunch concession. The ride has been in continuous operation in the same location since its installation, to the delight of generations of park visitors. The menagerie carousel's 48 animals, 3 chariots, and 1 rocking chair were driven by a steam engine; rides originally cost just a nickel.

In 1916, as his boardwalk operations grew, Trimper erected an additional area for rides and concessions further south on South Second Street and named his new development Luna Park. Son Granville C. Trimper joined the family business with the purchase and operation of a No. 12 Big Eli Ferris Wheel from the Eli Bridge Company of Jacksonville, Illinois. The other main attraction of the new Luna Park was the Whip; this new invention of the William F. Mangels Company was a great sensation when it debuted in Coney Island the season before. The Mangels Company ignited the ride industry by producing a line of smaller versions of the adult attractions suited to younger riders. Trimper embraced this new market and purchased several "kiddie" rides, such as a carousel, a waterless boat ride, a Ferris wheel, and a Fairy Whip. With the exception of the land boats—retired in recent years—the original set of kiddie rides still surrounds the large carousel. It is this collection of Daniel Trimper's rides that define Trimper's Rides and bring generation after generation back to the park to watch their children and grandchildren enjoy the same rides that thrilled them in childhood.

By being located so close to the ocean surf, the property had always been vulnerable to the ravishment of extreme weather. The aftermath of the great storm of 1933, however, would prove fortuitous for Trimper's and for Ocean City. The storm's high waters and damaging winds destroyed property and businesses as it cut an inlet through the town connecting the ocean to the bay. The Trimpers lost a large section of their property including the Whip building located at the southern end of island. Yet this newly formed inlet was seen as a great advantage to the fishing industry and the steps taken to ensure the inlet remained caused a widening of the beach in front of Trimper's, enhancing the property along the way.

In the 1950s, the Trimper family added outdoor rides. Granville C. Trimper had started his own ride business, taking his Ferris wheel and a few other rides on the road to carnivals in the late summer and off-season. Upon his death in 1953, his son, Granville D. Trimper, would operate some outdoor attractions on the property on a more permanent basis. Longtime Ocean City mayor Daniel Trimper Jr. had succeeded his father in running the park throughout the wartime years and beyond until his death in 1965. Leadership of the park was then handled by his son, Daniel Trimper III, and his nephew, Granville D. Trimper. After returning from service in World War II, Daniel III operated several successful business ventures before lending his expertise to the family business. In 1964, Granville teamed up with amusement artist Bill Tracy to create what has become an award-winning boardwalk icon—the Haunted House. This thrilling dark ride of illusion and chills combines the best of modern scare technology with the novel artistry that is Tracy's signature style. The pace of expansion increased in the mid-1960s, with a new ride being added nearly each year. The purchase of the land and rides of Melvin Amusements opened up the rest of the block to Baltimore Avenue, and the modern era of Trimper's Rides began to take shape.

By the early 1970s, the carousel was showing its age. The years of faithful service had taken its toll. The Trimper family decided to undertake a major restoration and hired brother and sister John and Maria Bilous to perform the work; the complete restoration project took three years. The cherished heirloom retains its magnificence now through regular retouching.

The public's appetite for faster, scarier, and more exciting attractions was answered with the addition of the double-loop boomerang roller coaster called the Tidal Wave. Compact and elegant, this thriller decorates the skyline for visitors crossing into town on the Route 50 Bridge. Trimper's Rides also boasts an equally delightful tradition of the best games of chance and skill, along with all the fun foods that go with a sun-filled day on the boardwalk.

Trimper's employees believe it is the sense of nostalgia that brings generation after generation back to the amusement park. This book pays tribute to the many people, events, and attractions that have made Trimper's Rides the unforgettable destination for family fun for over a century.

One

A LEAP OF FAITH

Daniel Trimper left his Baltimore saloon business in 1892 and moved to a town barely beyond the planning stages. The town was reached by train or boat and communication with the surrounding area was slow. With his wife, Margaret, at his side tending the hotels, he would quickly establish himself as the provider of amusements and showed his tenacity as he rebuilt his hotels multiple times after damaging storms. The purchase of the beautiful Herschell-Spillman Carousel in 1912 helped his "bowery" area of fortune-tellers, popcorn stands, and games of chance gain the more wholesome reputation for family entertainment that Trimper's Rides enjoys today. The first electric lights on the resort were created by the Trimper's Rides engines. The boardwalk, once a collection of boards laid on the sand and taken up by business owners and put on their porches each evening, was made into a more lasting walkway. His son and grandson would be sent off to World War I, both to return damaged by the effects of mustard gas. The Trimper family would own land and businesses in the downtown area, including, briefly, the Seaside Hotel. Daniel would hold public office, starting a family trend of service to the community. The kiddie rides in his Luna Park and carousel building firmly established the south end of the boardwalk as the amusement hub of the Ocean City.

Enterprising Prussian Daniel B. Trimper began life in America as a cigar maker and tobacconist in Baltimore in a home he shared with his mother, stepfather, and stepsiblings. The family operated several saloons in the German district (now home to major professional sports venues), and Trimper provided catering special events and popular steamer excursions as well as refreshment stands at local parks. He and his wife, Margaret, would have 10 children, only 7 of whom reached adulthood. His decision to move his remaining family from a thriving metropolis to the relative rusticity of early Ocean City would have a lasting effect of the fortunes of his family and the town. Remembered as a kind gentleman, Trimper served on the city council. His fierce commitment to the success of his adopted hometown went beyond his own business concerns. (Courtesy of Wendy Bruno-Trimper.)

No. 1102   LOOKING SOUTH FROM THE PIER, OCEAN CITY, MD.

Coyprighted 1906 by Geo. B. Conner.

The castle-like turrets on the facade of the Windsor Hotel rise above the stretch of concessions that comprise the Trimper family property in the early 1900s. Sea bathers share the sands with horseback riders a short distance into the breaking waves. Swimming costumes were rented at bathhouses like those found at the Eastern Shore Hotel, just north of the Windsor.

BOARD WALK AND PIER, OCEAN CITY, MD.

Vacationers are seen taking a stroll in front of the original merry-go-round building. The curved sign is just visible under the roofline. This early ride was first operated on manpower or pulled by live ponies. By late 1911, this building would be replaced in preparation for the new menagerie carousel.

Grandsons Daniel Herny "Goldie" Gordon and Howard Turner and son Granville Christopher Trimper play in front of the New Windsor Hotel, which was built to replace the Windsor Hotel that was wrecked by storms in 1904. Goldie and Granville would serve during World War I, where both would suffer effects of mustard gas attacks before returning to Ocean City.

The Trimpers quickly tied themselves to the area. Many of the family who did not join the amusement operation would go on to own successful businesses, hold high offices, and in other ways contribute greatly to the success of Ocean City. Tenacity, a call to service, and a deep devotion to community are all traits exhibited by the Trimpers and have helped them rebuild and grow with the town. (Courtesy of Wendy Bruno-Trimper.)

The bold wooden arch proclaims the entrance to the Windsor Resort property on the corner of South Division Street. Guests passing underneath would be met with the bustle of vendors and a host of exotic entertainments to sample.

No visit the seashore is complete without fresh saltwater taffy. The growing number of diversions, including bowling, skating, and motion pictures, within Windsor Resort guaranteed that is was a destination for nearly every visitor to the town, much as it is today.

This view of Windsor Resort reflects the extent of the amusement property during Daniel B. Trimper's lifetime. Under the pole-topped cupola to the right of the Windsor Hotel is the current home of the famous 1912 Herschell-Spillman Carousel. The fanciful facade of the Luna Park

touches the boundary at South Second Street that is the location of Harrison's Harbor Watch and the Ocean City Life-Saving Station Museum.

NEW AMUSEMENTS AND BOARD WALK, OCEAN CITY, MD.

As more hotels and guesthouses were being built, Trimper turned his focus to his area of expertise—family entertainment. With the opening of Trimper's Luna Park, he was able to expand his offering of rides, games, and refreshments and begin the association of the name Trimper with amusement park fun. However, the storm of 1933 slowed any additional thoughts of expansion for the next few decades.

Ferris Wheel and Swing, Ocean City, Md.

Granville C. Trimper's Big Eli Ferris Wheel offers riders new sensations and unique views as the ride reaches its peak. A collection of swing boats, or "lovers swings," was among the earliest rides added to Trimper's Luna Park.

THE WHIP AND FERRIS WHEEL, OCEAN CITY, MD.

William F. Mangels Company's popular new invention, the Whip, was added to the newly opened Luna Park. The absence of electricity meant that the ride had to be operated by a generator. The Trimpers would move the ride to a larger building that would also contain a roller rink. This building and the Whip itself were washed away during the storm of 1933. The beautiful rink flooring was saved and installed in the family home. Fortunately, the Ferris wheel had been repositioned closer to the Windsor Hotel and escaped critical damage. The Fairy Whip, a "kiddie" version of the Whip, still operates inside of Trimper's Rides. The car decorations and fencing surrounding the mini version are identical to the full-sized one seen here. Adults must now look on with envy while the little ones enjoy this timeless attraction.

A solitary soul braves the elements in front of the Windsor Resort property during the winter of 1918. The roof of the Pier Ballroom building in the distance collapsed following this storm. Pounding waves threaten to overwhelm the seawall constructed to save boardwalk properties. Many such storms forced the early entrepreneurs of Ocean City to rebuild their business, some many times over. (Courtesy of Wendy Bruno-Trimper.)

Boardwalk businesses have fallen prey to fire as well as to raging storms. The Trimpers' property narrowly escaped this 1929 fire. The structure still standing is the Eastern Shore Hotel on South Division Street. A larger, more destructive fire had destroyed much of the neighboring blocks only four years earlier. The brave efforts of the several fire companies in the area would save Trimper's Rides in the future when the Dough Roller burned in this same spot in 2008.

Two

THE CALM AFTER THE STORM

The creation of the inlet, with its boon to the fishing industry, and the building in 1952 of the Bay Bridge, connecting visitors from Baltimore and Washington, DC, with the seashore, rapidly increased the popularity of Ocean City as a resort. However, this resulted in very little change to the attractions offered at Trimper's. Wartime rationing and shortages were prohibitive to building; the only large project during this time was the construction of the Inlet Lodge Hotel in 1944. The next generation of Trimpers were starting families and branching out into other businesses. Popular mayor Daniel Trimper Jr. faced many challenges during his tenure, including ridding the island of slot machine and bingo gambling. During the war, the East Coast was vulnerable to attack from the German navy. Trimpers was forced to use 10-watt bulbs in shielded tin cans to provide illumination. After the war, decorated veteran Daniel Trimper III pursued business interests before stepping in to lend a hand in the family park when his father died in 1965. Granville D. Trimper was learning the carnival trade while working with his father, Granville C. Trimper, at Eastern Shore Amusements in addition to working for the family in summer; he soon would join his cousin to take Trimper's into the modern day.

This view of the boardwalk from South First Street looking north shows the property taking on a more permanent and unified shape. A variety of attractions filled the stands, including the winner-every-time favorite, the string game. Players would choose a single string from a group, give it a pull and reveal the prize tied to the end.

Maurice Wilkins mans the popular shooting gallery. Aspiring marksmen could get seven shots for a dime. The target fixture remains in place behind the track of the Kentucky Derby Game that now occupies this stand. Maurice and his wife, Betty Wilkins, ran several successful businesses, including the Surf Villa Hotel and the Cork Bar, a boardwalk favorite. Betty also served for many years on the board of Windsor Resort, Inc. (Courtesy of the Betty Wilkins family collection.)

Winners of the milk bottle game were able to choose from a surprising variety of prizes. Household wares were offered along with toys and novelty apparel. Likenesses of popular film characters, such as the Snow White doll on the upper shelf, make up the majority of the top-prize choices in games' merchandise today. (Courtesy of the Betty Wilkins family collection.)

AFTER FIVE DAYS RETURN TO
GRANVILLE TRIMPER
OCEAN CITY, MD.

FIREMEN'S
CARNIVAL

FUN FOR EVERYONE

JULY 1 To JULY 12

PRESENTED BY

Greensboro Vol. Fire Co., Inc.

GREENSBORO, MARYLAND

AND

Eastern Shore Attractions

G. TRIMPER   :=:   MILTON, DEL.

FOR YOUR ENTERTAINMENT
SOMETHING SPECIAL EACH NIGHT

Granville C. Trimper's Eastern Shore Attractions offered rides and amusements for hire at local events and carnivals. This poster (left) is from one of the local carnivals. These events featured fireworks, music acts, parades, and even women wrestlers in addition to the rides, games, and food. Granville C. Trimper's business stationery (above) evokes the fun and excitement of the carnival.

Young Granville D. Trimper met lovely Joanne Morgan (above) at the Sharptown Carnival (below) that was held on the grounds across from her father's gas station and the Morgan family home. The couple's children and grandchildren fill key roles in the management of Trimper's Rides today. At age 12, Granville became the youngest owner of a Big Eli Ferris Wheel. His father had arranged for him to obtain his own wheel after Granville Jr. had shown he was capable of the maintenance and operation of the ride. Eastern Shore Amusements would continue to travel the carnival circuit as well as operate out of the Windsor Resort property until the early 1950s, when its warehouse and several of its rides were destroyed by fire. Granville Sr. died in 1953, and his son decided to continue operations in Ocean City.

Daniel Trimper Jr. took the reins of the family business from 1929 until his death in 1965. A real community leader, he served as mayor, Worcester County commissioner, and was active in his church. One of the founding members of the Ocean City Volunteer Fire Company, he was also involved in many other businesses outside of Trimper's, including real estate, pile driving, marine construction, and railroads. (Courtesy of Wendy Bruno-Trimper.)

This inlet view shows Windsor Resort, Inc. property not long after World War II. The new Inlet Lodge, seen between the Windsor Hotel and the inlet, was built by Granville C. Trimper and was run by his wife, Pearl. With the expansion of the beach, the pounding surf, once only steps away from the boardwalk, was no longer a regular menace.

Mayor Daniel Trimper Jr. (left) plants an umbrella as part of a publicity campaign promoting Ocean City tourism. He served as mayor from 1944 to 1959. Upon his resignation, he was presented with the Distinguished Citizen of Maryland award for the growth and development of Ocean City.

Gambling was a growing problem for the resort as slot machines appeared in businesses all along the boardwalk. Mayor Dan Trimper Jr.'s administration worked with state police and county prosecutors to drive gambling out of Ocean City. The resort's reputation as a family destination subsequently grew.

The sky's the limit in this early children's airplane ride. Details such as a front propeller help to capture the rider's imagination. This ride is of the swing chair variety. The themed seats are suspended from the upper circle that turns as the cars swing outward. (Courtesy of the Betty Wilkins family collection.)

A new section of rooms has been added to the Inlet Lodge. The outside ride area can be seen next to the boardwalk entrance. It was once known as Inlet Casino, and ads for the Inlet Lodge encouraged guests to dance to the music of Tony Villani or Hank Clausen and his Hillbilly Orchestra. The porches on the bay side of the hotel take advantage of the sunset views.

The Tilt-A-Whirl is a carnival standard. This early version is one of many owned by the Trimpers over the years. The color schemes may change, but the basics of the ride still delight the daring.

The Octopus Ride is shown here with its decorative seats covered. Part of the Eastern Shore Amusements set of rides, the arms of this monster send riders on a disorienting journey as the seats spin, turn, and dive.

Daniel Trimper III was the president of Windsor Resort from his father Daniel Trimper Jr's death in 1965 until he retired in 1980. An avid sportsman, he enjoyed the boating, fishing, and society that Ocean City had to offer. Although he shied away from politics, he served the country in the Army Corps of Engineers during World War II and was decorated with the Purple Heart. (Courtesy of Wendy Bruno-Trimper.)

Trimper III partook in a number of very successful businesses, including the Trimper's Marine Railway, real estate, and a pile-driving venture. He was active in waterfowl and marine conservation, serving as deputy inspector for the state's conservation commission. (Courtesy of Wendy Bruno-Trimper.)

The creation of the inlet was a spectacular boost to the sports-fishing industry. Boats can travel quickly from the calm docks of the bay to deep-sea fishing in the ocean. Ocean City's marlin fishing attracts the top sportsmen in the world to town to compete.

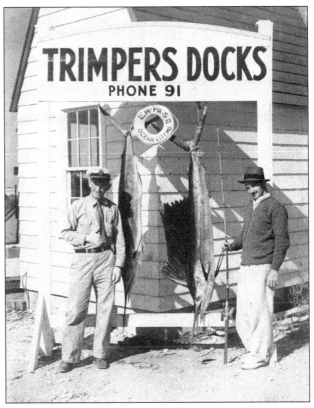

With the vast buildup of new beach in front of the property, the Trimpers offered the city the right-of-way for two rows of parking. This postcard shows the first rows and beginning of the inlet parking lot.

Granville Daniel Trimper served with Daniel Trimper III as vice president, taking over as president of Windsor Resort in 1980 until his death in 2008. Granville served on the city council for 18 years, many of them as president; he also served as mayor. In 2000, he was elected Citizen of the Year by the Ocean City Chamber of Commerce.

The ease of travel as a result of the opening of the Chesapeake Bay Bridge in 1952 meant that Ocean City's popularity as a vacation destination was increasing at a rapid pace. But a trip to the south end of the boardwalk still meant trying to win the largest teddy bear or following the sound of the carousel music.

Three

THE CAROUSEL BUILDING

A new structure was built in 1911 in anticipation of the arrival of the Herschell-Spillman Carousel. The carousel arrived by train disassembled; however, the Herschell-Spillman representative was called home, leaving Daniel B. Trimper, son Granville C. Trimper, and employees to assemble the ride on their own. The purchase of a selection of kiddie rides added to the appeal of the inside ride area. In the 1920s, the Trimpers were able to generate electricity to help power the rides and provide lighting. Some customers visited the park simply to enjoy the lights. The Trimpers were also able to sell electrical power to other businesses in Ocean City. The next large purchase was the Big Dodgem. Park lore tells that the original steam engine for the carousel was too large to be removed and was buried under the floor of the Dodgems when installed. The friendly Hampton umbrella rides were purchased in the 1970s to add to the number of offerings for little children, making the carousel building a must-visit spot for families coming to town. When the carousel lost some of its luster, the Trimpers decided to invest in a multiyear restoration. They hired a brother-and-sister team educated at the Maryland Institute College of Art in Baltimore to do the work. This section tours the inside rides and the restoration of the "Pride of the Boardwalk"—the Herschell-Spillman Carousel.

This ad from the Herschell-Spillman Company of North Tonawanda, New York, describes the advantages of its carousel offerings. The style, associated with carousels produced at this factory, is called Country Fair Style and features smaller but highly stylized horses.

This postcard shows the Trimper's carousel in earlier days. The house that surrounds this work of art was designed and constructed to feature the ride, which was originally steam driven and was converted to use electricity.

The Fairy Whip was manufactured by the W.F. Mangels Company of Coney Island. This ride is a child-sized version of the ride swept into the inlet during the August 1933 storm. Several newer attractions have adapted the whipping motion of the ride with different themes. Mangels understood that the anticipation was a large part of the fun.

The W.F. Mangels version of the Ferris wheel for children is designed to let riders enjoy the heights but also keeps them safely enclosed within the cabins. The fringed top of the land boat is seen in the foreground.

The waves are made of wooden track and the open seas of blue tarp, but these land boats offered high-seas adventure for generations of little captains. One of the original Daniel Trimper purchases, this old favorite was recently retired.

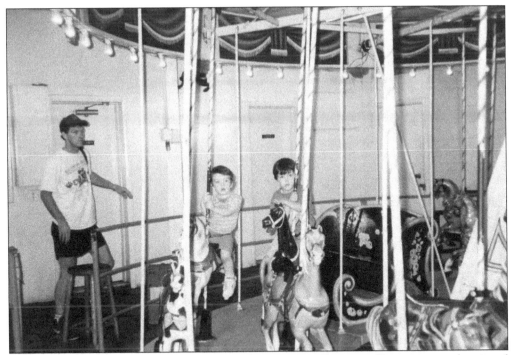

For those not quite ready for the big carousel, Trimper's offers a smaller version with painted ponies. This little gem was purchased from the W.F. Mangels Company in the 1920s.

The clang of the bells announces that the fire brigade is on the way. Purchased from the W.F. Mangels Company, the individual cars are named for local area fire departments.

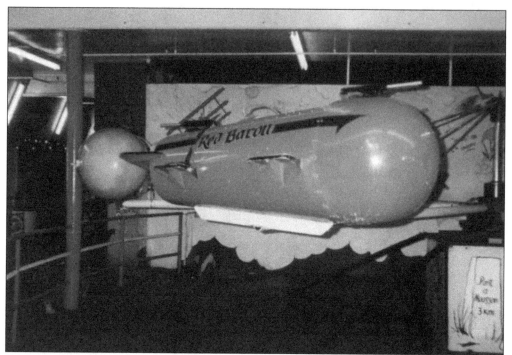

Generations of pilots have taken their first flight on this metal airplane ride. The mounted guns allow the heroes to thwart the enemy ahead or behind.

The boats take riders on a delightful journey by the docks of a seaside town filled with friendly faces. While a slower, gentler ride than the land boats, these boats have the added pleasure of being on the water.

The bumper cars, or Big Dodgems, are one of the few attractions for adults inside the carousel building. The bumper-lined center island keeps the flow of traffic close for more action. Shouts of joy are heard when young riders have finally grown tall enough to enter the fray.

For those too small for the Big Dodgems, this version provides a fun but sized-right experience for young riders. The Kiddie Dodgems have the more common open-floor style of play.

Young drivers have their choice of vehicle to hit the open road. Whether school bus, snowmobile, or sports car, the classic Hampton combination rides are crowd-pleasers.

One of the oldest forms of amusement park attractions, wacky mirrors were positioned in parks to delight visitors out for a stroll. Visitors walking the boardwalk can come to Trimper's to enjoy the simple silliness of the distorted image. For the best entertainment value in Ocean City, no ticket is required.

The sounds of the carousel music add to the nostalgic feel when on a visit to Trimper's. Originally, the music was provided by a band organ playing an assortment of scrolls, but the sea air makes it difficult to keep in tune. The Trimpers opted for a reel-to-reel tape system that has since given way to CDs. These unique instruments are a pleasure to look at long after their music has stopped.

The rides inside the carousel building are geared toward the youngest guests. The games featured also appeal to kids (and parents) with winner-every-time favorites like the Duck Pond. Pick a duck out of the gently flowing stream and a hidden number reveals the prize. While the Duck Pond was retired a few years back, the same game format applies to the Shark Attack.

The popularity of the Frog Bog game's mallet and catapult action inspired some variations, like this Scooby Bones game. The game was decorated to match the Scooby-Doo plush that was the prize.

This beautiful, ornate Victorian ticket booth was originally used as the main booth inside the building. Restored along with the carousel in the late 1970s, this heirloom booth is still functional and able to be called into service. Mathilda Burbage recalled that her grandmother Margaret Trimper used to say the "angel on top watches over the block."

Shooting galleries have been a feature of the park since the earliest days. This novelty gallery, with its fanciful critters, bottle targets and even a piano player to activate, greets customers entering the building on the South Division Street side.

By the 1970s, the carousel was starting to show its age. Although it has been repainted after World War II, the colors were becoming muted and muddied. The Trimpers chose to invest in a multiyear operation to restore the carousel and the antique ticket booth to their original splendor. These photographs illustrate the darker tones that hid the rides' true beauty. Brother-and-sister artists John and Maria Bilous were hired to complete the task. Neither had worked on a carousel before, so they conducted research into the colors, paints, and techniques used in the manufacture of these treasures. Each figure was removed from the ride and taken to the artists' work area for the process.

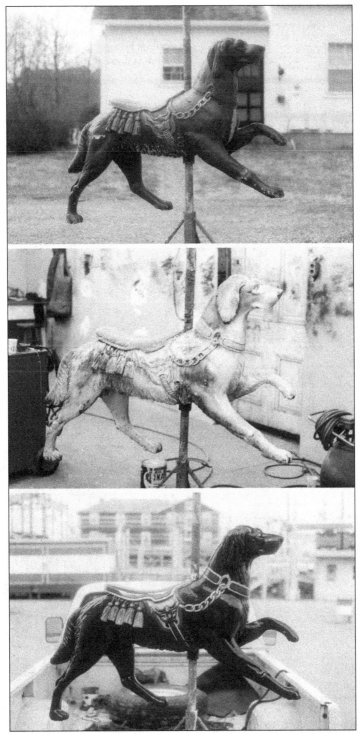

This panel illustrates the before, during, and after photographs taken during the restoration. The figure was stripped of the layers of paint down to the wood and any damage was repaired before the figure was given its fresh new look and returned to the ride.

The once faded stork has been returned to its original magnificence. The restored colors brought a lightness back to ride. Storks were not common figures on carousels.

Maria Bilous (now Schlick) gets up on a ladder to do the fine detail work required to bring these figures back to glory. Not all projects can come to her workspace. The trim on the platforms had to be completed on-site.

The carousel's animals were not all that needed attention. The chariots and rocking chair were due for some updating as well. In the background, the murals used to set the scene in the Kentucky Derby boardwalk game are being prepared for use as well.

Carousel figures are traditionally carved more ornately on the outside, or "show" side, of the piece. The relative plainness of the wood on the inside of the piece gave the artist the chance to enhance its beauty with paintings that echo its theme.

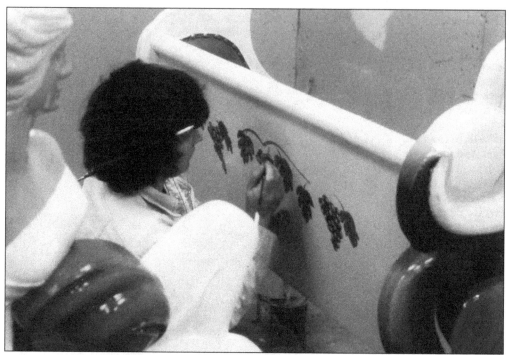

Maria's detail work magnifies the original beauty of the figures and adds much to the aesthetic pleasure for the riders. Often-overlooked surfaces can be an opportunity to make a piece more beautiful.

The 1912 Herschell-Spillman Carousel is shown after the restoration is complete. Measuring 50 feet in diameter, this three-row, two-level, park-style ride has 4 chariots and 48 animals, 23 of which are horses.

The rounding board has additional carvings, including a series of faces both human and animal. These gargoyles often go unobserved, but their watchful eyes seem to see all.

The restored figures show off the artistry of the original carvings. The horse's musculature, the individual tassels on the lattice blanket, and the radiance of the phoenix wings are brought to life. This photograph shows the scrollwork and painting done to the step between levels.

Carousel animals are described by leg and head positions. This pig from the innermost row is called a jumper because of its bent legs that look to be mid-jump and a stargazer to indicate that its head is looking up to the heavens.

The expressions in these figures' faces give a lifelike quality to the animals. The individuality of the figures contributes to this as well. The second giraffe is very similar but has a ribbon instead of tassels at the neck and his mouth is closed.

Among the original paintings decorating the center is a painting of the Windsor Resort from the time of its creation. Other paintings show fashions and landscapes; another panel promises free rides to the holder of the brass ring. However, this carousel does not have a brass ring feature.

Founder Daniel Trimper's favorite animal, the armored horse, is the most elaborately decorated, containing many jewels. This figure is ready to take the lead. Family lore tells that at his funeral, an arrangement of flowers was made in the shape and pattern of this particular horse.

The stationary wall of lighted mirror panels that surrounds the lower part of the carousel's motor was not part of the original ride purchase but was added at a later date. The extra lights and reflective surfaces contribute to the radiance.

Sargasso the Sea Monster is the only mythological creature on the carousel. Despite his piercing eyes and razor-sharp teeth and claws, small children often cannot wait to hop on his saddle and go for a ride.

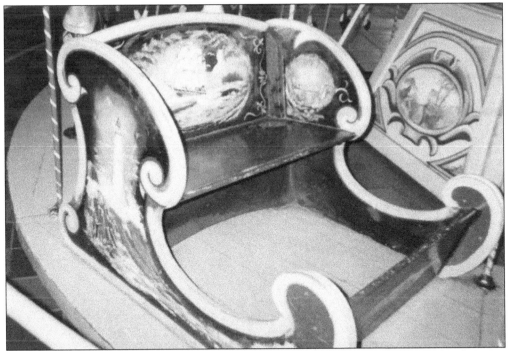

The small carousel also received fresh paint. While all of the horse figures are of a relatively simple design, the chariots and central panels provided a canvas for Maria to decorate and beautify as well.

Once plain surfaces like walls and benches are transformed into showpieces of their own. The mural of the Windsor Hotel is similar to the painting on the carousel and is another reminder of the wonderful history of the park.

The pair of Wild Mouse archway mice is readied for another season. When the ride was retired, one of these mice was preserved and displayed in the building.

The amusement park would be quickly overwhelmed if a large number of trash receptacles were not provided. The Trimpers lovingly maintain their fleet of vintage novelty trash cans, each a work of art.

Four

COME TAKE A DARK RIDE

Granville Trimper closely followed trends in the amusement industry. He decided it was time to add its first dark ride. He chose designer Bill Tracy, president of Outdoor Dimensional Display Co., Inc. out of Secaucus, New Jersey. Tracy visited Granville in Ocean City in late January 1964 to inspect the site, which was previously used as the Windsor Theater. Soon after, Tracy's artists would begin development of the iconic stunts and massive facade of Trimper's Haunted House. Tracy was on-site for the ride's installation. The ride opened to the public in 1964 and was an instant success. Tracy was invited back in 1971 to construct Pirates Cove, a walk-through–style funhouse attraction containing a nautical theme, complete with skeleton pirates, sharks, forced-perspective hallways, a maze, and obstacles that offer patrons the feeling of getting seasick on the boat deck.

During the winter of 1988, Granville expanded his popular Haunted House to two stories by incorporating the Tracy stunts he had acquired from the closed Playland Amusement Park. The ride reopened in the spring of 1989. From the ride's expansion in 1988 to present, the Trimper family has added effects to keep the ride fresh and exciting. In 2011, several additional Tracy stunts from Phantasmagoria at Bell's Amusement Park in Tulsa, Oklahoma, were incorporated into the ride over the winter. That same year, a complete renovation involving new stunts, updated lighting, and fresh paint was completed. Bill Tracy died in August 1974, but his attractions live on at Trimper's Rides. Granville Trimper and his family have always understood the value of their priceless Tracy rides and continue to take pride in keeping them exciting for generations to come.

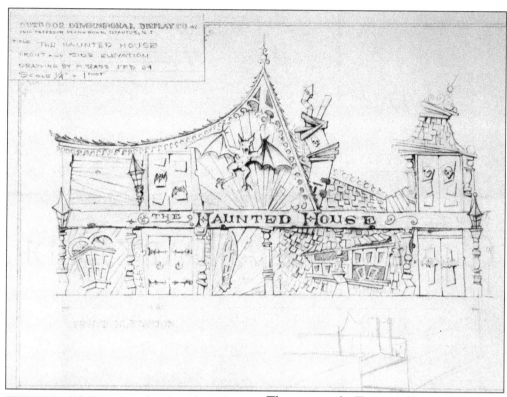

The concept for Trimper's Haunted House was developed by Bill Tracy of Outdoor Dimensional Display Co., Inc. The original drawing of the facade was hand drawn in February 1964 by Manfred Bass, an artist and sculptor who worked for Tracy in the early 1960s that is perhaps best known later in his career for his work as a float and balloon designer for the Macy's Thanksgiving Day Parade.

One of the first modern-day stunts to be added to the Haunted House was Count Wolf Von Vinderstein, a life-sized, animatronic barker installed in the ride's lobby. (Courtesy of Brandon Seidl.)

This photograph offers a close-up look at the ride a few years after the attraction first opened. The textured surfaces of the quirky facade are visible. Granville Trimper was able to expand the ride with remarkably little alteration to the overall look. (Courtesy of Olive Milutin.)

Ticket seller Annie Magee and ride manager Clifford Hudson are ready for guests to enter the Haunted House. Clifford's son, Scott Hudson, manages the ride today. (Courtesy of Olive Milutin.)

Cars are built with three-quarter-inch solid-core mahogany with pinewood overlays and carvings meant to resemble a combination of a four-poster bed and coffin. Their uniqueness is not limited to their appearance; to be able to showcase the stunts, the cars had to be designed to be able to negotiate tight turns, roller coaster–like dips, wave rooms, tilted rooms, and steep grades.

Bill Tracy's 'Tilted Corridor' illusion uses forced perspective, ultraviolet lighting, and a ramp that tips the coffin carriage off-center to offer patrons a sense of unreality. (Courtesy of Brandon Seidl.)

Trimper's Haunted House is one of the only Tracy dark rides to feature the "upside down room," a 16-by-16-foot room complete with furniture, lamps, and a helpless victim being awoken to chaos from a deep sleep. (Courtesy of Brandon Seidl.)

Tracy's scenes of horror are often served with a hint of salaciousness and a bit of humor thrown in for good measure. The attractive young victim's expression is more of surprise than terror, a subtle reminder that these frights are all in fun. (Courtesy of Brandon Seidl.)

The sweet old lady before the visitor turns to reveal the skeletonized character Knit-wit in a stunt reminiscent of Norman Bates's mother in the Alfred Hitchcock film *Psycho*. (Courtesy of Brandon Seidl.)

The torture chamber is another example of the Tracy style. The villain is unable to concentrate on his horrible task at hand as he ogles the helpless maiden. (Courtesy of Brandon Seidl.)

In 1981, another Tracy dark ride called Ghost Ship became available after Ocean Playland Amusement Park on Sixty-Fifth Street in Ocean City closed its gates for good. Granville Trimper jumped at the opportunity to acquire the defunct attraction, and after winning a high bid for the remains, he ventured to the abandoned ride with his crews to disassemble the interior of the attraction and bring the stunts back to his warehouse, where they would be stored for seven years.

During the winter of 1988, Granville made the decision to expand his popular dark ride to two stories by incorporating the Tracy stunts he had acquired from Ghost Ship into the ride. The expansion made the ride into one of the longest dark rides in the industry. He reimagined the ride carefully, considering placement of stunts and illusions. After a long winter of construction, a new Trimper's Haunted House opened its doors to the public in the spring of 1989.

Shown here is the seasick pirate as seen in the Ghost Ship ride before it was removed (above) and after as it was incorporated into the Haunted House (below).

This crab is another attraction from the Ghost Ship to be installed into the Haunted House. The scenery in front of him came from the Ghost Ship as well. The stunt was retired in 2006. (Courtesy of Brandon Seidl.)

The Haunted House came with indoor plumbing and the popular Last Drop stunt. The fun of this stunt is in the sound effects; the running water sounds and the plaintive cries for "Help!" produce tension-releasing laughs. (Courtesy of Brandon Seidl.)

The Train Tunnel effect came right out of Granville Trimper's idea bank. The illusion was furnished with the unused revolving barrel rock mold from the Ghost Ship acquisition. The park's artist painted the front end of a locomotive, and a light and sound were added to complete the effect. (Courtesy of Brandon Seidl.)

The Angel of Death is an impressive modern stunt illuminated by the full moon over his shoulder. This is just one of many new features added to the ride in recent years. (Courtesy of Brandon Seidl.)

The ominous tones of organ music emanate from the ride onto the boardwalk. With this new addition, riders can see who is making all that spooky music. (Courtesy of Brandon Seidl.)

Seen here is the facade of the Tracy-designed Pirates Cove as it was shortly after installation in 1971. The large orange Trimper Rides sign can be seen on the rooftop behind the attraction.

The drunken pirate room contains many of Tracy's signature elements. This fellow has clearly had too much rum and shows no signs of stopping any time soon.

This spinning vortex tunnel is purposefully both claustrophobic and disorienting. Tracy's attractions featured illusions and trick floors to give visitors many sensations while inside.

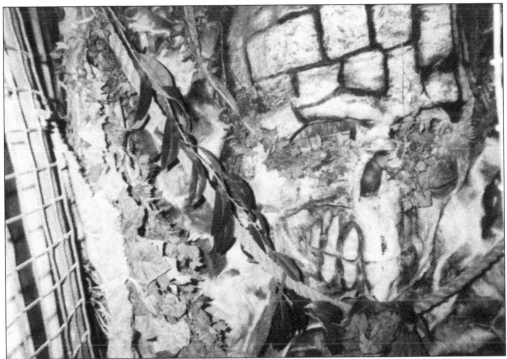

This giant skull made of stone seems to have been left by some ancient culture to ward off those who seek their secret treasures. Tracy attractions had a smattering of these larger sculptures to balance with the scenes and solitary figures.

This poor fellow is reduced to his bones, but he retains his eyes and the fashion sense to don a festive pirate hat. The fearful scenes are imbued with humor to relieve some of the tension.

A pair of animatronic birds who tell waiting guests about the fun and frights to be found inside the Pirates Cove have been added to attract riders. The seated pirate below the birds' nest is a popular photograph spot.

The Ghost Hole, another dark ride, called Trimper's home for a time. It had an impressive facade with nightmarish monsters and ghouls looking for their next victim. The ride found a new home on Coney Island.

Five

MIDWAY MAGIC

For many years, the name Trimper's Rides meant the carousel, the kiddie rides, and the Tilt-A-Whirl. The purchase of the land and rides from the operation next door allowed for the expansion into the rest of the block west to Baltimore Avenue. Granville Trimper convinced his cousin Daniel Trimper III to invite some ride owners to set up rides in the "back." The rapid expansion in the number of rides and attractions that followed was impressive. At first, the majority of outdoor rides were those commonly seen at a traveling carnival. The Trimpers replaced many of these with sturdier models designed for use in amusement parks. Making more rides fit in the limited space became a challenge and rides were often relocated within the park, the layout resembling a giant puzzle to be worked. People associate the inside rides with nostalgia, but it is never an easy decision to retire any of the rides. It is like saying good-bye to a valued friend. Many fun rides and games have come and gone. Later expansions included the purchase of Marty's Playland arcade and the construction of the Inlet Village shopping center. This chapter addresses the development of the outside ride area as well as the boardwalk attractions and a visit with a few old friends.

Customers are enjoying the go-carts in this photograph from 1970, taken before the installation of the Pirates Cove. Many of the attractions featured outside are booked in rather than permanently a part of Trimper's. Park offices were still located inside the carousel building.

The ride area next to the Inlet Lodge grows. A Merry Mixer and Loop-o-Plane have been added to the familiar Tilt-A-Whirl, Ferris wheel, and Octopus. While many of these attractions have been set up in different locations around the park, the Tilt-A-Whirl has always been at home on the boardwalk.

This unusual view of the Tilt-A-Whirl and the corner of South First Street comes from high up in the Zipper. Trimper's did not yet have permanent outside ticket booths when this photograph was taken. The small white box next to the Tilt served as a booth.

One of the most popular thrill rides in the history of Trimper's Rides, Chance Manufacturing's Zipper is the best at eliciting screams and riders' loose change. This most daring example of a whip-type ride allows riders to rock the seating cages to increase the dizziness.

The Turbo was another thrill ride from the Chance Manufacturing Company. This photograph shows the corner of South First Street and Baltimore Avenue. Two wheels spun back-to-back as riders in pods at the end of each spoke made the journey around the wheel.

The Rotor allowed potential riders to watch from above as those in the ride were spun in a carpeted drum fast enough to stay in place when the floor is dropped from beneath them. Variations on this same concept show up in rides like the Round Up and in the futuristic-looking Gravitron.

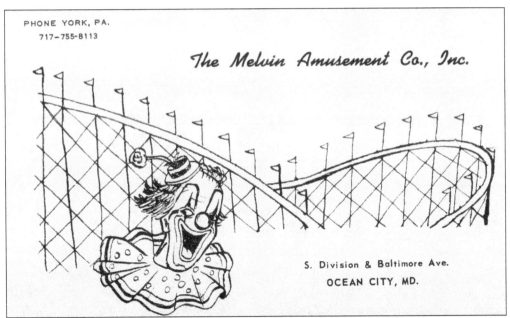

PHONE YORK, PA.
717-755-8113

The Melvin Amusement Co., Inc.

S. Division & Baltimore Ave.
OCEAN CITY, MD.

The Melvin Amusement Company operated a small collection of rides on the corner of South Division Street and Baltimore Avenue. In October 1970, Windsor Resort, Inc. agreed to purchase the rides, buildings, and equipment owned by Melvin Amusements. The purchase included the French Frolic, the Tempest, the Round Up, the Mirror Maze, and a roller coaster called the Wild Mouse.

Master electrician and maintenance chief Ralph Holloway operates the Round Up. One of the rides purchased from Melvin Amusements, the Round Up is a carnival staple that relies on the forces from the spinning platform to keep the riders in place along the perimeter.

The Loop-o-Plane stands tall across South Division Street from the Mirror Maze. The Mirror Maze was given a permanent structure in the construction project that expanded the Haunted House to two floors. The old Mirror Maze building has been repurposed as a maintenance supply room.

The Tempest was another carnival-type ride purchased from Melvin Amusements. Buying the additional rides and land greatly increased the number of outdoor rides owned by Windsor Resort and changed the shape of the park to include the whole lot behind the Windsor Boardwalk property back to Baltimore Avenue.

The Wild Mouse was a single-car roller coaster whose quick turns and quicker drops brought fear and delight in equal measure. These photographs are showing the ride as it is being dismantled to make way for the Tidal Wave. The two large fiberglass mice that pointed the way in have already been removed (above). In the image below, the zigzags and dips of the track are still in place.

This ad from the early 1970s has coupons aiming to promote daytime business. Trimper's Rides would eventually offer an afternoon special of a pay-one-price wristband for day customers.

Stephanie Trimper Lewis sells tickets in one of the now permanent white brick ticket booths with the brightly colored light-up sign indicating tickets for sale. The list of outside rides has had many changes in the years since this was taken.

The Merry Mixer moved from the area next to the Inlet Lodge to its current location within the "back" of the park. The Yoyo swing ride is running full loads on this early evening in summer. The Yoyo would be moved to the north end underneath the Tidal Wave before being sold and being replaced by the Wipeout.

Games were also a feature of the back of the park. The Apple Dart game was next to the Pirates Cove. A winning smile and an outgoing personality go a long way to making a successful games cashier.

The Toboggan from Chance Manufacturing was a unique type of single-car roller coaster. The two-seater car was hauled up to the top of the tower section and then would spiral around the outside on the bright red track until just before the bottom, where it would complete a section of dips before returning to the station. The Toboggan was regretfully retired after many great years of service when Trimper's could no longer get parts to care for the massive chain inside the tube.

The Olympic Bobs, a ride from Chance Manufacturing featuring a Swiss theme, was designed to resemble bobsled cars racing up and down an icy track. The operators are resting on one of the bobsled cars. As the number of attractions increased, the need for summer staff also increased. The British Universities North America Club, or BUNAC, offered a work-and-travel program, allowing British students to obtain temporary work visas to earn money for travel around the United States. Trimper's was one of the first businesses to participate in the program.

The Mini-Telecombat allows young flyers to choose whether their space saucer or plane flies up or turns close to the ground. Meant for small children, the ride looks so fun that the operators want to give it a try.

Young or young-at-heart riders still enjoy a spin of the Tilt-A-Whirl by Sellner Manufacturing Company of Faribalt, Minnesota. This 1965 model replaced a 1940s model that operated in the same spot.

Seen here is Trimper's Rides and Amusements as it was during Sunfest of 1983. This unique aerial view from the boardwalk side of the property shows the circular roof of the carousel building; the outline of the Eastern Shore Hotel is visible to the right. The snowy white mountain circle in the

center of the image is the Olympic Bobs. The buildings across the boardwalk from the rides are Souvenir City and House of Pasta, with Steve's Carryout below. The restaurants were operated by the Trattner family. (Photograph by Paul J. Smith.)

Games of skill were the norm through much of the history of Ocean City. As the town became a family destination, the appetite for racing-style games where family members could compete with each other grew in popularity.

The Cobra ride from the 1970s was positioned at the north end of the park next to the Aladdin's Lamp funhouse. Could it have escaped the snake charmer's basket?

Similar to the Hampton combination rides found inside the carousel building, the Hampton motorcycle ride was a step up in action; the motorcycles execute a jump and pop wheelies on their way around the circle. The white rocket on its side in the background is the simulator ride, called the Astroliner. Riders entered the rocket and watched a short movie while the operator rocked and tilted the ride to match the screen action.

This is a great view of the Car Rack game, a carnival standard. Players throw balls to try to tip over a certain number of the cats or "punks" to claim the prize. This game was located in a trailer by the Wild Mouse.

This overhead view of the back of Trimper's Rides was taken in the mid-1980s. The Inlet Village has been built on the south side of the Inlet Lodge.

From left to right, Mathilda Burbage, Granville Trimper, Glen Schlick, and William Burbage sit together on a bench in front of the Pirates Cove. Granville and ride owner Glen Schlick could be seen on this bench through the evening in summer. Mathilda served on the board of Windsor Resort, Inc. with her cousin Granville. They each loved to see the customers having a good time and kept a watchful eye over operations.

The Water Flume at Trimper's was one of the first water parks in Ocean City. The flume has two lanes that feed into a small landing pool. A system of different colored mats helps lifeguards keep track of when a rider's time had expired.

The Space Shuttle ride was a mid-sized boat-swing ride operated in the park in the mid-1980s. A smaller boat swing, the Pirate Ship, was operated in the park a few seasons later. The park's latest big boat ride is the Rocking Tug; not a swing ride, this boat privets and surges with realistic sea-tossed motion.

This photograph of the Aladdin's Lamp funhouse shows the huge genie who bows his head from his seat atop the ride entrance. This Arabian Nights–themed walk-through attraction was recently refurbished. The ride's footprint was reduced by nearly half, yet all the original stunts were incorporated in the new design.

The Bowler Roller game requires the right touch to roll a bowling ball over the hump but without so much force that it rolls back. The water-race game Bullseye currently occupies this concession.

Riders on the Skywheel, a double Ferris wheel, experienced breathtaking views to match the breathtaking free-fall. The Whac-A-Mole trailer was moved next to the Merry Mixer to build a Frog Bog game. The music ride, the Matterhorn, would switch places with it sister ride, the Himalaya.

The Frog Bog game is a modern classic seen here after its installation in the late 1980s. Players would use a mallet to launch a rubber frog from the catapult, aiming to land it in a lily pad. Families gathered to watch the fun and enjoy the music from the Matterhorn.

Amusement Ride "Boomerang"
Vergnügungsanlage "Boomerang"

MORGAN HUGHES, INC.
140 Sylvan Avenue
Englewood Cliffs, New Jersey 07632
Vekoma international bv
(201) 947-8800

VEKOMA

Granville Trimper needed to find a thrilling ride that would fit into the space limitations of the park. He chose the Boomerang roller coaster, made by Dutch ride manufacturer Vekoma, and named his version the Tidal Wave.

After the Wild Mouse ride was dismantled, foundations were set in preparation for the Tidal Wave to be erected. The Olympic Bobs and the Round Up were also sold to make room for the exciting purchase.

Larry Wisdom (left) of Wisdom Industries and security guard Ronald Mears overlook the pieces of track that are being laid out for assembly. The ride has an off-season maintenance schedule for both the track and the train itself.

The cresting wave section of the Tidal Wave is nearly complete. The ride would be ready to open in the summer of 1986. Several years later, the coaster would undergo scheduled metal refurbishment and portions of the track would be again removed to undergo the treatment. The sight of the missing part of track caused some fans to fear that the ride was being removed.

Granville Trimper takes the first ride on the Tidal Wave. The game across from the ride platform is a Pacman-themed game. It was traditional for Granville and staff members to try the new attractions before opening up for the public.

The train is hauled backwards up to the top of the first lift and then released, sending the train back through the station and into the twisting wave section. Riders brave enough to keep their eyes open receive a great view of Ocean City as the train gets taken higher.

The train
continues through
a vertical loop
and is then hauled
up to the top of
the second lift
and released to
repeat the series
of loops in the
opposite direction
before returning
to the station.

Smiles are all around as the Tidal Wave's first official ride comes to an end. The joy was short-lived when the ride was found to overhang the sidewalk, in violation of city ordinances. The Trimpers were forced to cut a five-foot section and half of the inspection platform from the ride with no guarantee it would be able to operate in the new configuration. To everyone's relief, the Tidal Wave was good as new and opened to much acclaim. Also visible in this photograph is the Gravitron, the spaceship-like ride in the center of the image.

The dazzling lights, the cheers and screams, and the rumble underfoot as the Tidal Wave roars through the station all come together to mean a perfect summer night at Trimper's Rides. Resembling a German village storefront, the Charlie's Hat game offered a uniquely charming spin on the target shooting experience. Moving platforms with life-sized figures of men wearing hats would spin by the player, who must knock off a number of hats to win the prize. Also shown are parents gathered around to watch their little ones pilot fanciful spaceships on the Viking ride, seen here next to the blur of the Cycles.

This postcard gives a nice look from both directions of the boardwalk in front of Trimper's Rides. The top section shows the Red Apple concession stand in the corner. The collection of apartments above was added in 1967 and incorporated the remains of the Easter Shore Hotel. Originally leasing to a variety of tenants, the apartments today are primarily employee housing for the foreign work-exchange students.

A fancy sign hangs over the shooting gallery on the boardwalk in this image from the 1970s. When the gallery closed, the sign was re-tasked to advertise the shooting gallery just inside the South Division Street entrance to the carousel building.

The Kentucky Derby racehorse game is one of the most popular games ever operated at Trimper's Rides. Contestants roll a ball on the playing surface, hoping it will land in a high-scoring hole to advance the horse. Crowds gather as the excitement builds to hear the announcer call the race and proclaim a winner.

This lucky lad has won the top prize in the Balloon Race game. The original water gun game requires players to shoot a stream of water into the clown's mouth to inflate a balloon. The first contestant to pop the balloon wins the race. Boardwalk strollers are often startled by the loud pop that signals the winner.

In the jungle, the mighty jungle, the Lion Race game is a family favorite enjoyed by many looking to take home a fun, plush wild-animal prize.

A clever spin on the milk-bottle game, Gun Ball used a plastic baseball with a stopper that could be shot out of a gun and aimed at a pyramid of plastic cylinders. The player needed to knock all three cups off the table to win the tuxedoed flamingo.

Can Alley is themed for the younger set. Brightly colored plastic balls are thrown into an opening-and-closing trash can by contestants hoping to reach the winning total ahead of the competition.

Big prizes can be won by anyone with the skills to shoot out the star on this Target Gun game. Players would get 100 shots to try to obliterate the red star from the center of a small target. Located just beyond the vintage Pepsi machine is the original Del's Lemonade cart at Trimper's. Lemonade operations moved to the large fiberglass lemon-shaped stands. (Courtesy of Brenda Runk Parker.)

Replacing the Target Gun was a custom-designed Whac-A-Mole game. This version is in addition to the Whac-A-Mole trailer in the back of the park. Rules and game play are the same for both, but the prize mix varies. Unlike the single-player versions of the game where the object is to best a high score, these park versions are a race game in which competitors try to be the first to score 150 points. The game has reached cultural prominence with references appearing in popular TV shows, music videos, and political sound bites. (Courtesy of Brandon Seidl.)

A balcony overlooking the boardwalk was added to the apartments located on the corner of South First Street. This addition extended the row of multicolored lighting panels that so many people associate with Trimper's on the boardwalk. Many of the concessions on this end of the property were operated by George and Pete Haas, including the Ship Store and Souvenir City gift shop. Now run by Robert Auker and his family, Souvenir City and Inlet Gifts have just the thing for those looking to take home a memento of their visit to Ocean City. (Courtesy of Olive Milutin.)

The Carousel Corner gift shop was next to the boardwalk entrance to the carousel building and offered carousel-themed gifts, Trimper's Rides souvenirs, and miniature replicas of several of the animals on the Trimper's carousel. These products are now sold on the Trimper's website. The decorative window added just the right touch.

This postcard shows vacationers passing next to the Red Apple concession stand heading north. The vintage Marty's Playland sign is visible in the distance.

Marty's Playland arcade was founded in the 1940s by Marty and Anna Mitnick. Anna's son-in-law Sam Gaffin ran the operation until retirement and sold the operation to the Trimper family. Marty's Playland has the same combination of cutting-edge attractions and nostalgia that makes the amusement park so popular.

Video games of every sort, vintage digger cranes, and pinball machines old and new fill row after row of the always bustling boardwalk arcade. As the Skee-Ball lanes kick out streams of tickets, customer start adding to see if they finally have enough coupons to claim the prize at the redemption station (above). Flashy coin falls, classic bowler games, and redemption games provide hours of enjoyment and prizes to take home.

The Water Flume was replaced by Tank Battle. Each tank had a driver and a gunner. The tanks would drive around an arena as other customers shot rubber balls from mounted guns along the arena fence. The gunner's supply of ammo is used to intimidate the other tanks or menace the perimeter shooters.

One of the first rides to be "booked in" at Trimper's in the early 1970s, the Matterhorn had already had an impressive run at the iconic Palisades Park prior to that park's closure in 1971. Owner Glen Schlick had taken the ride for many winters on the carnival circuit before calling Ocean City its permanent home. Glen's talented wife, Maria Schlick, painted the figures that decorate the top and center. Music styles changed from Top 40 pop to 1980s hard rock, then to hip-hop and R&B before going for the last spin.

"Do you want to go faster?" The fans respond with a resounding "Yeah!" The ride kicks into the next level amidst pounding music and a dazzling light show. Purchased in 1976 by a company consisting of Glen Schlick, Daniel Trimper III, and Granville Trimper, the Himalaya has been entertaining crowds both on the ride and those just standing around it to enjoy the atmosphere. A favorite feature of the Himalaya is that the ride operates in both directions. The cars travel into the alpine-themed tunnel section (below), emerging into the lights bouncing off the center mirrored ball. Starting in the late 1970s, groups of teens would gather along the curb in front of the ride on South First Street, nicknamed "Freak Street," to meet with friends and listen to the latest rock music. Groups still gather at the ride to enjoy the scene, but today it is families watching Dad trying out his best dance moves to the delight and shame of his giggling children.

Trimper's began to look for more family-friendly rides where children and parents could ride together. Zamperla's Mini-Tea Cup ride fit the bill. The riders sit inside a teacup around a center circle. The amount of spin is up to the individual riders. Cheerful and bright, the Tea Cups replaced the kids-only Viking.

Another family-friendly addition is the balloon ride Up, Up, and Away. Riders sit in basket-like seats and imagine they are heading for the clouds. The Motorcycle ride was moved inside the carousel building to join the other Hampton vehicle rides before it was retired from the park a few years later. (Courtesy of Brandon Seidl.)

This view from the Tidal Wave shows the Kiddie Bumper Boat pool. Beloved by children, the ride was dreaded by employees who needed to wade through the pool to assist the little ship captains. The Himalaya is seen in its current location after switching places with the Matterhorn.

A loving brother takes care to secure his little sister before the launch of the Sooper Jet, a kiddie roller coaster. The seemingly simple circular track still has enough thrills for a first roller coaster.

In the shadow of the Toboggan sits the Frog Hopper, a bouncing kiddie ride that introduces many young riders to the thrill of heights. Trimper's Frog Hopper has been renamed Russell's Frogs in honor of customer's favorite and perennial Employee of the Year Russell Sylvester.

Flying through the clouds in formation ready for battle, the Flying Tigers by Zamperla is a whip-style ride with the airplane-shaped cars suspended from above rather than rolling along a track. The Mini Telecombat was stored until it was added to the new Freakout lot.

The Yoyo spent a few seasons under the wave of the Tidal Wave until it was sold and the Wipeout (pictured) was put in the space. The surf's up and the seas are rough for the strong stomachs that brave the waves of the Wipeout.

Pirate chic is never out of style. Located at the exit of the Pirate Ship, the Top Glo water-race game delivers themed prizes for the first to have the column reach the top.

Space at the park has always been limited and challenges the Trimpers to find rides and attractions to fit into unusual spaces. The Rio Grande Train ride was a solution to the problem of the columns that support the Tidal Wave. The train operated for several relatively quiet seasons underneath the roller coaster until some more innovative thinking would bring this charmer into the spotlight.

Wisdom Rides Avalanche takes its place behind the Zipper, next to the Inlet Lodge A ride called the Gee Whiz that was booked in for a year to test the ride prior to the purchase of the similar Avalanche. This rainbow-colored family ride offers a fun sensation by swirling riders around sideways.

Chance Manufacturing's Inverter lives up to its name as riders get an upside-down view of the fun below. The ride is a variation on the flying carpet/boat–style thrill ride. Trimper's retired the Inverter after the 2013 season.

A tall tower-drop ride, the Sling Shot spent a few seasons in the Ghost Hole/Go-Kart track position. The ride was sold and replaced with a basketball game.

Inflatable attractions are becoming popular choices in the amusement industry. The Titanic inflatable slide was Trimper's first inflatable. The 2013 season introduced two others: a shark slide and the Mad Labs play area. Next to the Ferris wheel, the Speedball game is a guess-your-pitch skill game. However, many do not play to win the prize; the fun of seeing how fast they can pitch is all the reward they want. By 2002, the Pirate Ship had moved next to the Tidal Wave. (Courtesy of Brandon Seidl.)

Adventures await treasure hunters and high-seas pirates on the soft play activity slides the Raiders (above) and the Pirate Ship (below). These open-air funhouses allow kids to actively participate in the fun. Perhaps the little Raiders today no longer imagine they are Indiana Jones or even Lara Croft, but they don't have to imagine they are having fun. Kids need their sea legs to survive the rocking motion of the deck of the Pirate Ship. The funhouse has cannon blasts to ward off the giant octopus that has taken hold of the ship in shark-infested waters.

Granville Trimper owned the lot across South Division Street from the park and operated some rental properties there. In the mid-1980s, he opened a miniature golf course on the property. The course had an unostentatious city-park feeling to its design. Woe to those fooled by the simplicity of the layout—the individual holes offered excellent challenges. A few nights a season, the course would stay open late for employee golf night. The desire for more space for rides caused Granville and his family to dismantle the course.

The golf course office was managed by Jack Jarvis. When the ride area was constructed, the office was converted into a ride-ticket booth. The trapdoor for the ball return can still be seen in the floor of the booth.

The well-travelled Ferris wheel is in its final location on the brand-new Freakout lot. The Baja Buggy Jump-Around by Zamperla takes riders on an action-packed buggy ride over imaginary dunes.

Under the colorful flower-shaped lights is a long, green fellow with a funny face. He takes thrilled youngsters on a roller coaster ride. This medium-sized coaster is popular with those who are not quite (or never will be) ready for the Tidal Wave.

The new area offers games as well as rides. The guess-your-pitch Speedball, a basketball game, and the unique Four-in-One are all part of the fun. Four-in-One allows the customer to choose from a variety of games including some vintage boardwalk favorites like Darts and the String Game. A spooky new shooting gallery from the Scare Factory called the Haunted Parlor opened on the lot in 2013.

The Monster Mile of the Dover International Speedway is just over an hour away, but little race fans can get the best racing action on the Speedway at Trimper's Rides. This whip-style ride has the authentic look of NASCAR and is another family-friendly ride from Zamperla.

The happy, smiling faces on the seats of the Puppy Ride delight riders on this gentle flyer modeled after the Dumbo ride in the Disney parks

The crown jewel of the new section and the most thrilling addition to Trimper's since the Tidal Wave, the Freakout is a hit with riders and spectators alike. The mesmerizing pendulum swing of the center column gives way to the rotation of the claw-like seat section. This is what summer is supposed to feel like.

Time had come for the Matterhorn to retire, but Trimper's Rides would not be the same without a Matterhorn-type ride to offer to guests. The Trimpers decided on Bertazzon's Rock & Roll Matterhorn ride. The classic cruiser look of the cars enhances the jukebox and music note imagery of the scenery.

In 2012, two rides from the carousel building were slated to retire: the Motorcycles and the antique Land Boats. When a visit to the trade show did not produce a solution, the Trimpers got creative. Inspired by the effectiveness of the elaborate scenery at the Disney parks, Stephanie Trimper Lewis suggested they build a themed environment around the train ride they already owned. Over the off-season that year, the Trimpers collaborated on the biggest change to the carousel building in decades. The new train ride passes a working waterfall that flows over a mine tunnel (below) before entering the Wild West town and returning to the Granville Station. Animals and plants dot the landscape. These enhancements worked, making the new train ride is a huge success.

Windsor Resort, Inc. looked into other opportunities to expand operations. The Inlet Village of shops was built on the south side of Inlet Lodge. Trimper's Rides operated three stores, and several family members were the original tenants. Rusty Anchor sold brass and nautical novelty items.

Stuffed animals and cheer could be found in Toyland. The shops were designed like an old fishing village. Extra touches like flower boxes created a small-town feeling.

Nikki's Casual's merchandiser Mark Starliper selects a sweater to add to his display. His talents did not end with merchandising; Starliper was the cover artist for the menus at the Inlet Lodge Coffee Shop.

Located at the southern tip of the boardwalk, the Inlet Village also has fine dining in Harrison's Harbor Watch restaurant, seen on the right side of this photograph. The Ocean City Life-Saving Station Museum is the white building straight ahead.

The simple neon sign points the way with one word: *Bar*. The Inlet Lodge's ocean-view balcony used the same colored panels to signal that it was part of the Trimper family as well. In this boardwalk view, one of the boardwalk trains is starting up the boardwalk toward Souvenir City.

Full of large benches and long tables enjoyed by groups, the Bar is popular with employees who are of age. Karaoke night is held in the back of the room next to the stage. The Lodge has not had live music for many years. The end-of-summer staff party has been held here since the closing of the Water Flume.

The Inlet Lodge Coffee Shop has the nostalgic feel of an old-fashioned soda fountain. The hotel was originally run by Granville C. Trimper's wife, Pearl Trimper (pictured). Her son Granville D. Trimper and his wife, Joanne Trimper, took over after Pearl Trimper died.

The coffee shop serves food all day, but the crowd comes in at breakfast. Omelets, waffles, and fried eggs with scrapple prepared home style keep them coming back.

Nervous couples and glamorous gals in front of painted backdrops of fake scenery: since the beginning of Daniel B. Trimper's amusement area, there have been photographic studios. Customers would sit for a portrait that could be used as a postcard. The current Trimper's Rides includes Olde Towne Photo Emporium. Props include a getaway car, a fake bar, and a full-sized stagecoach.

Popcorn, cotton candy, snow cones are the basic food groups of fun in the sun. The Red Apple has been offering sweet treats for decades. Though it is named for the bright-red candy apples, the corner stand is best known for its funnel-cake creations.

Six

TRIMPER LIFE

The Trimper's Rides extended family grows every year with each new wave of students and new fans. There have been second-generation workers, as some have sought to spend the summer in the place their parents enjoyed working. Though the majority of the staff is seasonal, most are eager to return in spring to be part of the Trimper's team again. Social events, some spontaneous and some planned, generate a togetherness that keeps spirits high and smiles bright. Trimper's Rides and its employees give back to the community in more ways than attracting business to the town. Charitable work such as supporting Toys for Tots, autism awareness, and the Believe in Tomorrow House by the Sea Foundation and participation in the community is important to the company and staff members. There is a tradition of public service and involvement in civic organizations that goes back to the founder. Members of each generation of the Trimper family have been active participants in the community by holding leadership roles in public office, community groups, church offices, and in school volunteerism. Former employees have gone on to be successful business leaders, such as Matt and Mark Odachowski of Royal Plus. By hosting staff from all over the world, Trimper's employees get to learn about other cultures and share what is best about America in return.

Wheels of Yesterday car museum was founded by Granville Trimper. A labor of love, the museum had over 30 exhibits, including a re-creation of a service station belonging to his father–in-law, Joe Morgan, in the 1950s. After Granville's death, the museum closed and many of the cars and artifacts were sold to other enthusiasts who shared his passion for classic cars.

For a small, family-owned museum,
Wheels of Yesterday was highly regarded.
The collection included early models,
sports cars, and working vehicles.

Jack Benny's 1917 Overland was on
display in the Wheels of Yesterday
car museum. Docent Jack Jarvis
conducted personal tours of the facility,
offering anecdotes and insights into
the many treasures collected here.

Until it was sold in 2013, the Sea Isle Motel had been a location for employee-housing rentals. Many students reside in the apartments above the carousel building. Trimper's employees build lifelong friendships and have lasting memories of their experiences in the United States. Social events like themed costume parties, international buffets, trips to Frontier Town, midnight soccer in the inlet parking lot, and karaoke night at the Lodge are an important part of making the experience fun and meaningful for the staff.

Social events do not end with the season. Fall and winter mean more free time for the staff who have worked so hard all summer. Halloween parties, winter cruises, and staff reunions in England are some of the ways the family atmosphere at Trimper's stays alive.

The day after
Labor Day is
the date of the
end-of-season
staff party.
Originally held
at the Water
Flume ride, the
party offers food
and fun and a
chance to teach
the students the
proper way to
eat a Maryland
blue crab.

Some last pictures and smiles are captured before the students make ready for their next journey.
In the years since the flume has closed, the party has been held at the Inlet Lodge. A new tradition
of awards, gifts, and door prizes make it a fun, festive day and gives a chance for Trimper's to say
"thank you."

Special happenings can make a regular day at Trimper's an extraordinary one. This ceremony was to celebrate the release of a set of beautiful carousel-animal US postage stamps. Trimper's has also been the location for films shot in the area. *Violets are Blue* and *Ping Pong Summer* both had scenes filmed at Trimper's.

The Trimper's staff takes pride in the parades and events in the local community. The Trimper's friendly Dog character leads the float down the boardwalk during the May Parade.

Who knew Frosty worked at Trimper's? The staff participates in multiple Christmas parades in local towns. The collection of costumed characters accompanying the float brings out the smiles of summer on the faces in the crowd.

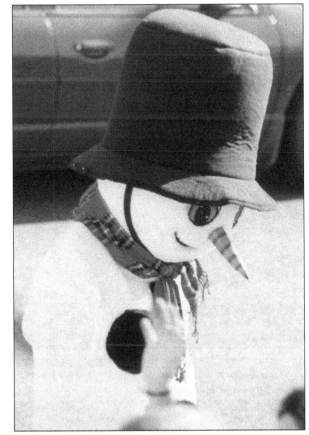

The Trimper's Rides' float brings Christmas cheer to the annual Ocean City Christmas Parade. One of the carousel chariots is playing the role of sleigh on this float. Trimper's has been fortunate to win a collection of trophies for its entries in the parades over the years.

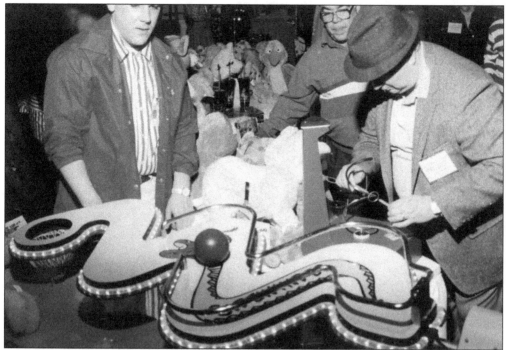

The Trimper's Rides family also participates in charity events and school fundraisers, and offers support through donations and sponsorship. Joseph Johnson monitors the action as event participants try out the games.

Fire crews from several local towns work tirelessly to contain the fire at the Dough Roller Restaurant that threatens to destroy neighboring Marty's Playland in 2008. Daniel B. Trimper and his son Daniel Trimper Jr. participated in the founding of the Ocean City Volunteer Fire Company; since then, many generations of family and staff have served and continue to do this vital work in the community. Trimper's Rides is proud to have so many fire company members in the family.

This collectible can was part of a promotion of Pepsi as "America's Hometown Choice." The campaign featured local spots of interest. Trimper's Rides was highlighted using the iconic image of the Toboggan roller coaster.

If asked, she will say she is "just the secretary." However, to the many students a long way from home, she is their den mother; to the Elmo plush who has lost an eye, she is the surgeon; but to most, Johnnie Jett is simply the heart of Trimper's Rides.

Visit us at
arcadiapublishing.com

CPSIA information can be obtained
at www.ICGtesting.com
Printed in the USA
LVHW062040060120
642667LV00013B/330/P

9 781531 673284